B O L D P R I N T

Bugs!

EDDIE GEORGE ING

Editorial Board
David Booth • Joan Green • Jack Booth

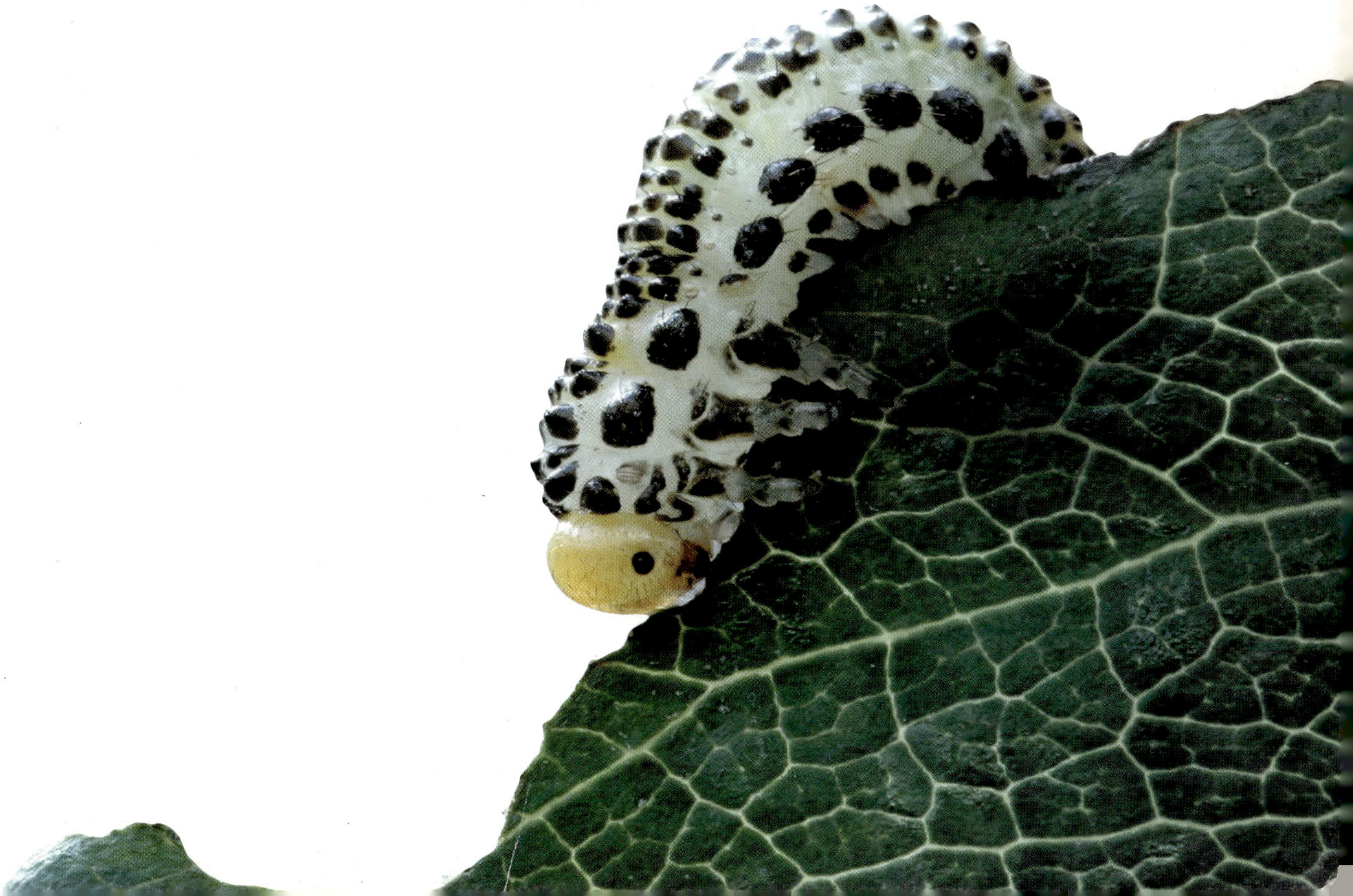

This book is dedicated to:

My loving wife, Patricia Jill Ing,
my parents, Debra-Anne Ing,
Kinfone Eddie Ing, and Edith Lamb,
and my brother Jason Ing.

STECK-VAUGHN
Harcourt Achieve

www.HarcourtAchieve.com

10801 N. Mopac Expressway
Building # 3
Austin, TX 78759
1.800.531.5015

Steck-Vaughn is a trademark of Harcourt Achieve Inc. registered in the United States of America and/or other jurisdictions. All inquiries should be mailed to Harcourt Achieve Inc., P.O. Box 27010, Austin, TX 78755.

Rubicon © 2006 Rubicon Publishing Inc.

www.rubiconpublishing.com

All rights reserved. No part of this publication may be reproduced or transmitted in any form or by any means, electronic or mechanical, including photocopying, recording, taping, or any information storage and retrieval system, without permission in writing from the copyright owner.

Project Editors: Miriam Bardswich, Kim Koh
Editorial Assistant: Kermin Bhot
Art/Creative Director: Jennifer Drew-Tremblay
Assistant Art Director: Jen Harvey
Designer: Kerri Knibb

6 7 8 9 10 5 4 3 2 1

Bugs!
ISBN 1-41902-382-9

CONTENTS

4 **Introduction**

6 **Is It an Insect?**
Did you know that not all bugs are insects? Read this article and find out how to identify an insect.

8 **Believe It or Not: Amazing Bugs**
Amazing creepy, crawly facts.

11 **The Grasshopper and the Ant**
A fable about how an ant showed a grasshopper a thing or two about hard work.

14 **Bloodthirsty Bugs!**
A report on bloodsucking bugs!

18 **Bug Jokes**
Did you know bugs can be funny? Have a laugh with these jokes.

20 **Champions of Bug Olympics**
Meet four famous bug athletes in this article.

24 **Little Miss Muffet**
A popular nursery rhyme about a girl who doesn't like spiders.

26 **Spot the Bugs in This Pond**
Search the picture for water bugs.

28 **Ronnie and Dribble's Wild Adventure**
A graphic story about two ants who were lost ... and then found.

32 **Investigate Ants**
An as-complete-as-can-be guide to ants and their homes.

38 **Amy's Mealworm Tacos**
A lip-smacking recipe for those who like to eat insects.

40 **How Much Lunch Can a Caterpillar Munch?**
A scientific experiment to find out how much a caterpillar eats.

42 **Splat!**
Drivers all over Britain have been counting bugs smooshed on their cars. Read this article to find out why.

44 **Tuna Bugwiches**
A fun recipe that shows you how to make delicious sandwiches.

Caterpillar previous page–istockphoto

Why I Don't Brush My Teeth Anymore

By Kij Johnson

I'm alone in the bathroom. A bug sidles up.

"That toothpaste sure smells tasty." It leers.

"Mmmmm," I say, brushing.

"You sure got a lot of toothpaste there."

"Mmmmm," I say.

"But then, there are sure a lot of us bugs," it says.

"Mmmmm," I spit.

"More than there are of you," it says.

"Help yourself," I say, and back from the bathroom.

---

sidles: *creeps up*
leers: *looks slyly*

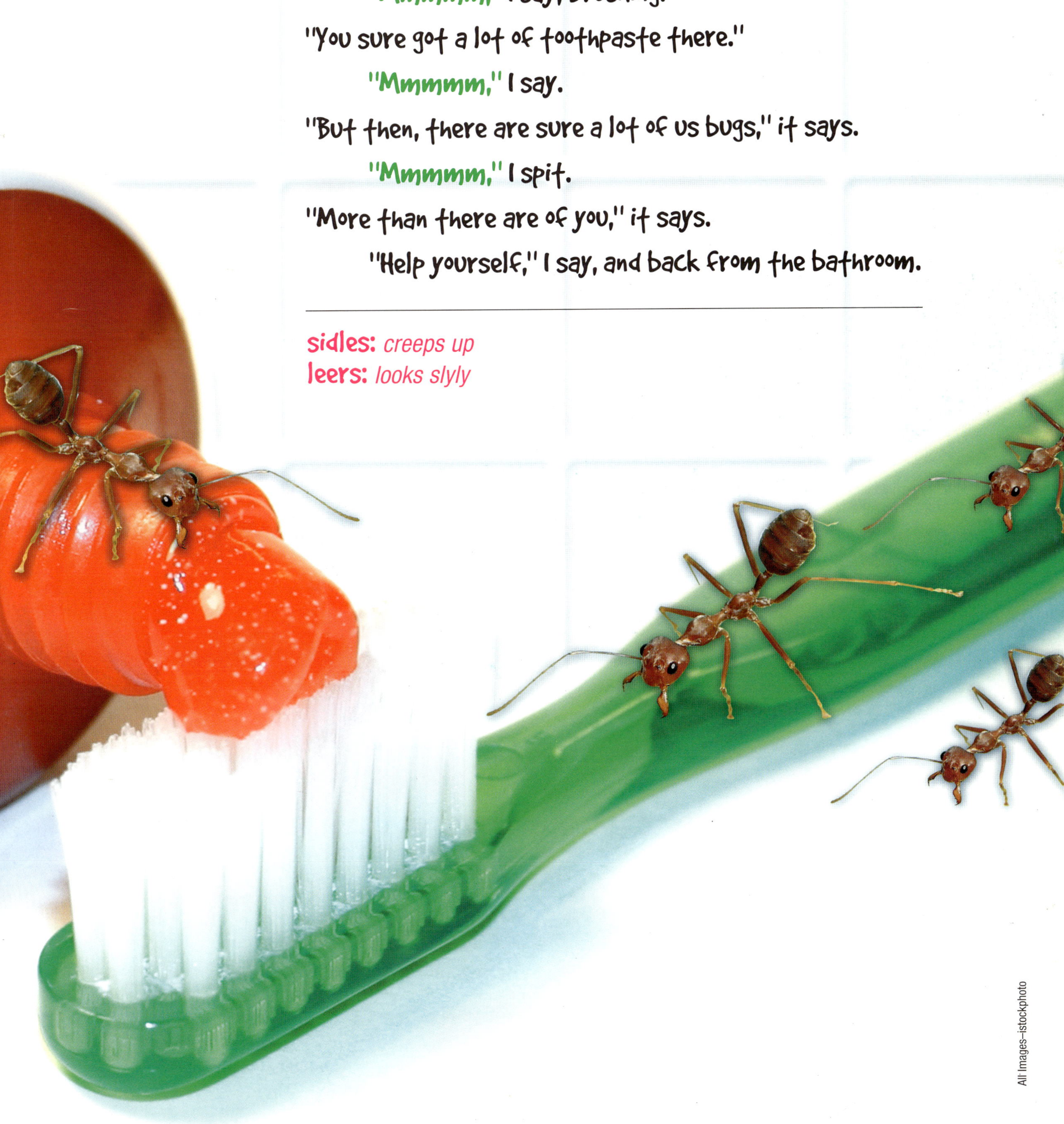

All Images–istockphoto

warm up

Even though they are small, insects seem to frighten many people. Why do you think this is so?

Is It an

We call all creepy, crawly things bugs. But not all bugs are insects. For example, spiders, slugs, or worms may look like insects, but they are not. So what's an insect and what isn't? There are four important clues to look for when figuring this out.

All fully-grown insects have:

- six legs
- three main body parts: head, thorax, and abdomen
- two feelers on their head called antennae
- one or two pairs of wings

Insects do not have bones inside their bodies. To protect their soft insides, they have a tough outer skin. It is called an exoskeleton.

All Images—istockphoto

Insect?

thorax
head
abdomen
antennae

wrap up

In a small group, brainstorm a list of all the bugs you know. Now try to figure out if they belong to the insect family.

WEB CONNECTIONS

Visit **http://www.pestworldforkids.org/home.html** to learn how insects can turn into pests inside a house. Make a list of all the pests and suggest ways to get rid of each one.

Believe It or Not: Amazing Bugs

warm up

Scan the pictures and name all the insects on these three pages. How many do you recognize?

Mantids are the only insects that can turn their heads around to look in all directions.

Earthworms are high in protein and low in fat. They are used in China to make a soup that helps stop pain.

The diving beetle tucks a bubble of air under its wings so it can breathe underwater.

Butterfly–Getty Images/OS18069; All other insects–istockphoto

Praying mantis–Getty Images/OS50083; Getty Images/OS50084; All other insects–istockphoto

wrap up

Use the above information to create "bug cards." Gather all the bug cards into a bug box and give it to your school librarian.

Background Images–istockphoto

The Grasshopper and the Ant

An Aesop's Fable

warm up

Do you do your chores or homework before you play? Take a poll to find out the work-play habits of the class.

All through the summer, my family and I worked hard gathering food for the winter months. Our family of ants worked harder than some insects in our neighborhood. In fact, many of the critters and insects around us seemed to think that summer was a time for playing.

FYI

A fable is a story that teaches a lesson. Aesop is a writer famous for his fables. This fable is one of his most popular.

One day, I was walking home when I passed by Mr. Grasshopper. He was singing and playing his fiddle. He stopped to talk to me. "Mr. Ant, why do you and your family work so hard? Don't you know that summer is the time when the sun is out the longest? We have to enjoy this wonderful time!"

"I know, Mr. Grasshopper," I replied. "But I only celebrate when my work is done. And my work is not done! I have to gather food so my family won't starve in the cold winter months."

"Mr. Ant, you sound like a wise old fool to me, even though you are much younger than me," said Mr. Grasshopper.

I paid no attention to his comments and went on my way.

Near the end of summer, the days and nights seemed to melt into one another. Our family's hard work was paying off. We had stored a mountain of food for the winter months.

CHECK-POINT
What do you think this sentence means?

Soon, winter arrived. The land was covered with snow and ice. There was no food to be found anywhere. Our family was as snug as a bug in a rug. We passed our time underground playing games, dancing, and singing by the fireside. We had plenty to eat.

One day, we heard a weak knock on the door.

"Mr. Ant," said Mr. Grasshopper, when I opened the door. "I'm cold, weak, and hungry. I am begging you … can you please give me some of the food you have saved?"

"This is not Mr. Ant," I replied. "This is the Wise Old Fool speaking! I'm afraid we have no food to spare."

CHECKPOINT

Why do you think Mr. Ant replied this way?

wrap up

1. Do you think Mr. Grasshopper learned his lesson? With a partner, discuss the lesson.
2. Complete the story by writing a paragraph explaining what happened the following summer.

WEB CONNECTIONS

Visit **www.umass.edu/aesop/contents.html** to read more of Aesop's fables. Pick your favorite and read it aloud in class.

Background Image–istockphoto

Bloodthirsty BUGS!

warm up

Many people are grossed out when they see blood. What are some things that make you feel sick just by looking at them?

Have you ever smashed a mosquito and found blood spurting out of it? If so, you have just stopped the mosquito from dining on your blood!

Many different insects live on blood. Fleas, mosquitoes, bedbugs, mites, and ticks all feed on blood from human beings and animals. These tiny insects suck up blood till they almost burst. Then they wait till their next mealtime to suck some more!

CHECKPOINT

Notice that we say one "louse" and many "lice" – just like we say one mouse and many mice.

FYI

To remove a tick, take a pair of tweezers and slowly pull the body of the tick. If you pull too hard, the head may stay behind.

TICK BITING DOG'S SKIN

The human louse feeds on the blood of human beings — usually blood from the scalp. Lice use their sharp mouths to poke into the scalp. Then they suck up blood. The head louse lives its whole life in human hair. Its eggs (also called "nits") stick onto hair. The average lifetime of a female louse is one month. During that time she can lay as many as 250 eggs! The eggs hatch in about a week. Like its parents, the young louse quickly pierces the scalp and enjoys its first meal of blood.

Most mites and ticks are less than .04 in. in length. After stuffing themselves on blood, they grow much bigger. Ticks eat only three times in their life. They feed on blood during each step of their three-stage cycle.

CHECKPOINT

Why do ticks and lice need blood?

All Images–istockphoto

Life Cycle of a TICK

Stage 1

A female tick lays eggs on grass. Six-legged larvae hatch from the eggs. They crawl up the grass blades and wait for an animal or a human being to pass by. The larvae then stick onto a passing animal, push their sharp mouths under the skin, and dig in for a feast. The larvae then "pig out" for a couple of days. Their bellies get bigger and bigger, like giant balloons. They then fall off and digest their first meal.

---

larvae: *baby insects*

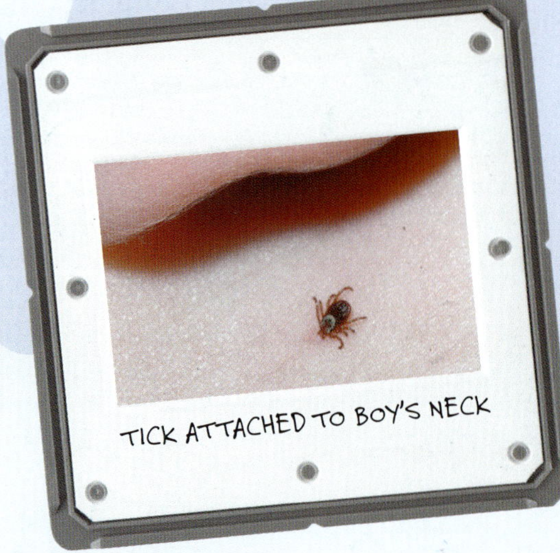

TICK ATTACHED TO BOY'S NECK

FYI

- A dog may return with hundreds of ticks after a walk in a tick-infested area.
- Before chemical treatments were invented to get rid of lice, nits were removed by picking through each strand of hair. People who are very fussy are therefore called "nitpicky."

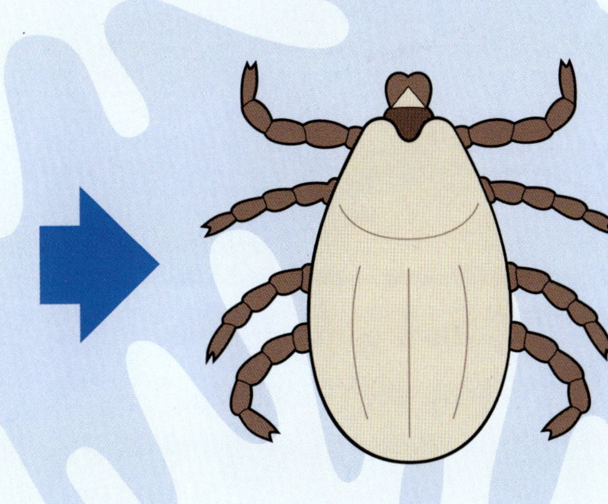

NYMPH

ADULT

Stage 2

The larvae grow into eight-legged teenage ticks or nymphs. The nymphs find another animal to feed on. They then have their second meal. They feed for several days. After that they drop off, digest their meal, and turn into adults.

Stage 3

Once that happens, it's time for their third and final meal. After this, the ticks are ready to mate and lay eggs.

---

mate: *produce young ones*

PREGNANT TICK UPSIDE DOWN

wrap up

1. Ask your school nurse what harm lice can do to your hair and health. Share your findings with the class.
2. Ticks only eat three times in their three-stage cycle. Imagine we human beings could only eat as a child, a teenager, and an adult. What three meals would you eat? Write a list of at least five items for each meal.

All Images–istockphoto

Bug Jokes

By Tracy Trimpe

Q What game do ants play with elephants?

A Squash!

Q What do insects learn at school?

A Moth-matics!

Illustrations by—Natalie Tweedie

Q What are the smartest bees?

A Spelling Bees!

Q What did one firefly say to the other?

A "I gotta glow!"

Q Why did the insect get kicked out of the park?

A He was a litterbug!

Q Who is the favorite singer for bees?

A Sting!

Q Why do bees hum?

A 'Cuz they forgot the words!

Q What goes "hum-choo, hum-choo"?

A A bee with a cold!

Q What goes "zzub, zzub, zzub"?

A A bee flying backwards!

wrap up

With a friend, write your own bug joke. Gather all the jokes from the class and create a book of bug jokes. Give it your own title.

Q What do you call a nervous insect?

A A jitterbug!

Champions of Bug Olympics

warm up

Have you ever thought of competing in the Olympics? Which sport would you play?

Trophy—Corbis

In 1992, Daniel Dragonfly won a gold medal in the wing-flapping competition. He vibrated his large wings 1,600 times per second to win the title. Daniel's friends call him "Helicopter" because he can fly in all directions up to a speed of 28 mph. He has 30,000 lenses in each eye. This means he can see in many directions. Once he left pond life, he started to train for the Olympics.

vibrated: *moved back and forth*

Daniel "Helicopter" Dragonfly

Monica the Monarch Butterfly

In 1996, Monica the Monarch Butterfly set a record while flying from Mexico to Canada. Her bright orange and black wings were a stunning sight. Born as an egg in a milkweed plant in the United States, Monica soon hatched into a caterpillar. She hung herself under a leaf by spinning a silk hangar for herself. Then her skin split to form a hard shell called a "chrysalis." Twelve days later, she changed into a butterfly and her Olympic journey began.

hangar: *shelter to live in*

Insect Images–istockphoto

Ricky the Rhinoceros Beetle

Ricky is a well-known name in the weightlifting world. In 2000, he lifted over 850 times his own weight to win a gold medal. Ricky is over 2 in. long. He uses the curved horn on his head to lift things. Having lived his entire life in a coconut palm tree, Ricky has decided to retire and live in the tropics.

In recent years, Graham's hearing has started to disappear. Despite his recent difficulties, he won the long jump gold medal in the 2004 Olympics. He used his 900 leg muscles to jump over 30 in.

Graham the Grasshopper

All Images–istockphoto

OTHER INSECT RECORDS

Bulkiest Insect

Goliath Beetle — 4.3 in. long, weighing 3.5 oz

Largest Water Insect

Giant Water Bug from Venezuela and Brazil — 4.7 in. long

Fastest Flying Insect

Hawk Moth — reaches top speeds of 34 mph

Most Poisonous Insect

Wasps/Bees — about 40,000 people are killed each year by their stings

Most Destructive

Locusts — a swarm can eat 20,000 tons of crops per day

Tallest Nests

African and Australian Termite — the nest can be up to 39 ft. in height

Loudest Communicator

Cicada — humans can hear its song from nearly 0.62 miles away

Toughest Insect

Snow Flea — remains active at temperatures colder than 5°F

Most Eggs Laid by an Insect

Queen Termite — she can lay 40,000 eggs per day

wrap up

Create a set of cards and name them "The Olympic Cards." Write something about the insect on the back of the card and draw a picture on the front. You could include information like name, size, habitat, year of Olympic competition, event entered, etc.

WEB CONNECTIONS

Visit **www.pixar.com/featurefilms/abl/** to find out how the movie *A Bug's Life* was made. Discover how Pixar Animation Studios filmed real bugs to understand the world from a bug's point of view.

warm up

Share stories with your class about people you know who fear insects.

FYI

Spiders are not insects, as many people believe. Insects have three body parts and six legs. However, spiders have two body parts and eight legs.

Spiders eat many types of harmful insects, helping to keep gardens free of pests.

Little Miss Muffet

Little Miss Muffet
Sat on a tuffet,
Eating her curds and whey;
Along came a spider,
Who sat down beside her
And frightened Miss Muffet away.

wrap up

1. Find out what "curds" and "whey" mean.
2. What is your favorite insect? Write a short poem about it.

Spider Webs–istockphoto; Spider–Getty Images/OS18073

Spot the Bugs in This Pond

Ponds are perfect homes for many small creatures. They are often nurseries for young insects too. Can you spot 121 minibeasts in this North American pond?

Fisher spiders crawl down plants, catch fish, then haul them up to eat. Spot eight.

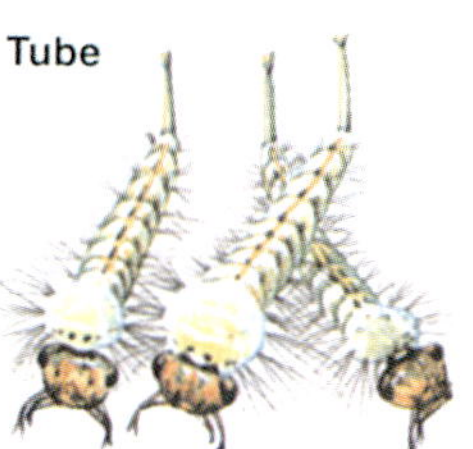

Mosquito larvae dangle under the surface of the pond. They breathe through a tube. Spot seven.

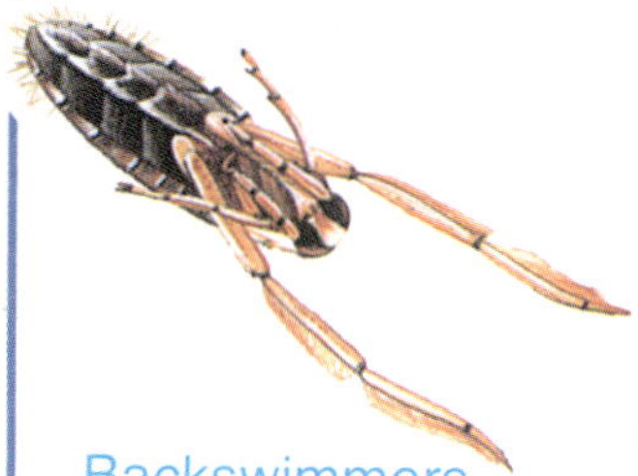

Backswimmers swim upside down, using their back legs as oars. Find six.

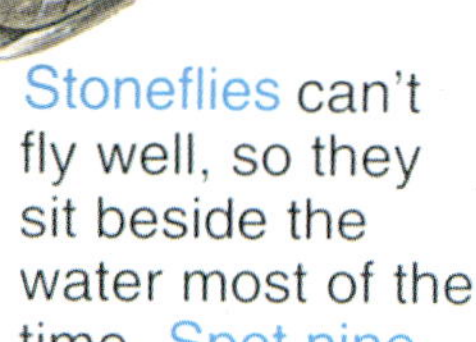

Stoneflies can't fly well, so they sit beside the water most of the time. Spot nine.

Damselflies can't walk well. They use their legs to grab hold of plants. Spot seven.

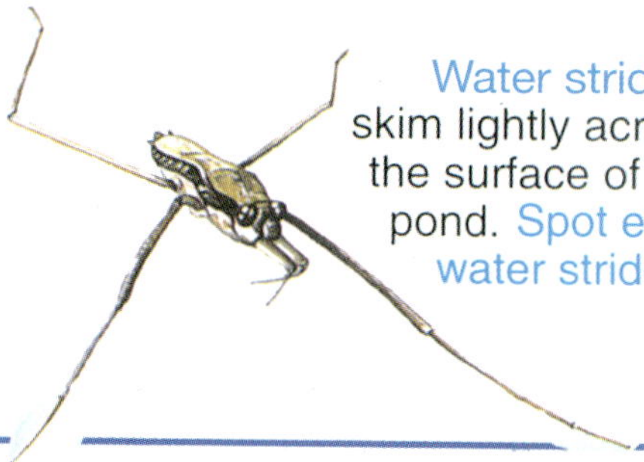

Water striders skim lightly across the surface of the pond. Spot eight water striders.

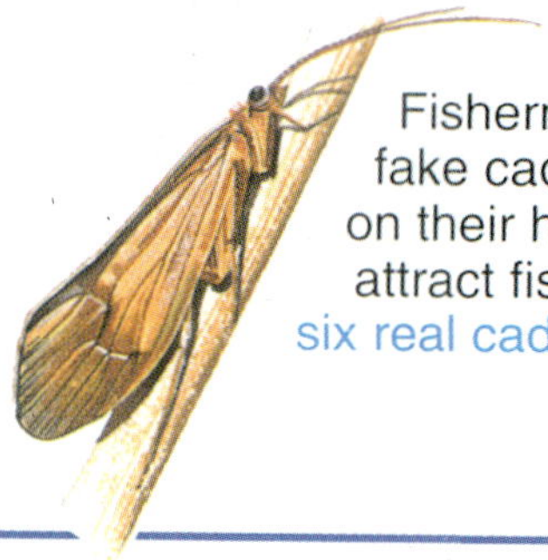

Fishermen put fake caddisflies on their hooks to attract fish. Spot six real caddisflies.

nurseries: *places that help things to grow and develop*

oars: *paddles*

Pond snails do a very useful job. They eat plants and make the water much clearer. Find 11.

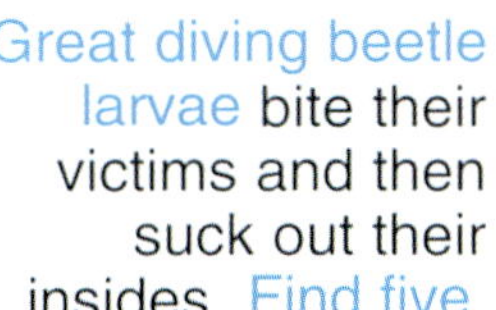

Great diving beetle larvae bite their victims and then suck out their insides. Find five.

Water scorpions lurk just below the surface, grabbing passing insects. Spot six.

Dragonfly nymphs have jaws that shoot out to crunch up food. Can you spot five?

Caddisfly larvae are safe inside a case covered with pebbles and shells. Find five.

Whirligig beetles can look into the air and under the water at the same time. Find 15.

Great diving beetles have strong back legs to help them swim and dive. Spot ten.

Water stick insects breathe air through a narrow breathing tube. Find five stick insects.

Adult mayflies never eat. They just mate, lay eggs and die. Find nine.

lurk: *wait out of sight*

Illustrated by FENWICK TIMMINS

RONNIE! DRIBBLE!

UMPFFF!!!

CRASH!
WHEW! THAT WAS A CLOSE ONE!!

SEE THAT BIG BOWL, DRIBBLE? IT LOOKS SAFE. LET'S HIDE IN THERE!

IT'S COZY IN HERE, RONNIE!
MMM, AND IT TASTES GREAT, TOO! I LOVE FRUIT SALAD!

HUH???
HURRY UP DEAR! I'VE SET THE TABLE.

WHY ARE WE MOVING? RONNIE! WHERE ARE YOU?
I'M HERE -- UNDER A CHERRY! JUST HANG ON! OH, I FEEL DIZZY!

IT'S SO BRIGHT HERE! I WANT TO GO HOME! I'M CRAWLING OUT OF HERE RIGHT NOW!
DRIBBLE DON'T! IT'S TOO DANGEROUS! ... WE HAVE TO FIND ANOTHER WAY!

HELLO!
EXCUSE ME! CAN YOU HELP US? WE'RE LOST AND WE NEED TO GET BACK HOME!

SERVES YOU RIGHT FOR FOOLING AROUND! WHAT STUNT ARE YOU TWO TRYING TO PULL?
OH NO, IT'S NOT LIKE THAT!
WE DIDN'T DO ANY-THING!
WELL, IT'S TOO DANGEROUS FOR ME TO HANG AROUND HERE!
HONESTLY! SOME PEOPLE'S LARVAE ...

BRRR! IT'S GETTING SO COLD! (SNIFF) I WANT MY DADDY!
HANG TOUGH, DRIBBLE! DON'T GIVE UP YET!

PASS THE FRUIT SALAD, HON. I'VE BEEN EYEING IT ALL AFTERNOON!
OF COURSE, DEAR. HERE, USE THE BIG LADLE!

AAAAHHH!!!

EWWW! BUGS IN THE FRUIT SALAD! HORRID BEASTS!

GET LOST!

AAAHHH!!!

wrap up

Pretend you are either Ronnie or Dribble. Write a journal entry describing your scary adventure.

Investigate ANTS

— Excerpt from *Investigates: Ants*

warm up

Have you ever been bitten by ants? Share stories with your group.

thorax with six legs and sometimes a pair of wings

head with big jaws, eyes, and antennae

long antenna used for smelling

jaws, called mandibles

FYI

There are more ants than any other creature on Earth. They are found everywhere on land except the polar regions.

For every human in the world, there are one million ants.

Illustrations by Michel Poirier

Living in Armor

An ant's body has three main parts: a head, a thorax, and an abdomen. The hard exoskeleton protects an ant's softer internal organs, including its muscles. The muscles move the hinges joining the separate parts of the exoskeleton. It is similar in design to some big machines, like cranes, giving tiny ants great strength to lift big, heavy weights. It would be like a little girl or boy easily lifting a car.

---

internal: *inner*
hinges: *flexible joints*

spiracles for breathing

sting

waist

two claws for grip

All Shapes and Sizes

Ants can be thin and long, or fat and short, depending on how they live. Most have black, brown, or dull-colored bodies. Some ants are brightly colored — usually as a warning to other creatures that they are dangerous. Apart from their strong jaws, which they can use to bite, some ants have a sting that can inject painful acid.

Ant Colony

Soldier Ants
Worker ants resting.
Winged new queens and male ants wait to fly away.
The large queen in her chamber lays eggs. The workers look after her and her eggs.
The chambers are connected by many tunnels.
Ants store their food in many chambers throughout the nest.
Nursery chambers are where the babies feed and grow.
Some chambers are used for dumping garbage.

FYI

Ants have poor eyesight. They use the antennae on their heads to help them find their way around. They are used for feeling, smelling, picking up vibrations, and taking the temperature.

Living Together

All the hard work ants have to do, like building nests, hunting, and rearing babies, is too much work for just one type of ant. Over time, ants have evolved several body shapes and sizes, called castes, to do these different jobs.

CHECKPOINT

Think it's weird that all the eggs hatch into females? Read the last paragraph on this page for more information.

CHECKPOINT

Why are worker ants important to the colony?

An Organized Life

Every nest has one large **queen ant**. She lays all of the colony's eggs. The eggs hatch into grub-like larvae. The larvae will grow into adult females, either as smaller workers or as soldiers.

The **workers** are what you normally see running along trails. They have many jobs, such as looking after the queen and the larvae, finding food, and building nests.

Soldiers are larger-sized workers. They often have bigger jaws, to hunt and defend the nest.

All the ants live together in many chambers or rooms in one nest. There are special rooms for the queen and her eggs, for the larvae, for storing food, and for the workers to relax. About once a year, the queen lays some eggs that grow up as new queens and male ants, both of which have wings to fly off to start new nests.

FYI

Once food is found, an ant lays down a scent as it returns to the nest. Other ants will pick up this scent and follow the trail to the food.

---

rearing: *looking after*
evolved: *developed or changed slowly*

Building a New Nest

Fierce weaver ants of Australia and Africa live among branches and patrol big territories, hunting all other insects for food. When the number of ants in one colony reaches a certain size, many workers and soldiers move out to build a new nest.

They start by forming living bridges, or ropes, forcing the leaves together. Other workers walk along where the leaves touch, and glue them together using silk in a zigzag weaving action.

After the first leaves are joined, the ants find more leaves to add to the final oval-shaped home. The ants do not get tired or bored, so a whole nest can be built in just a few hours.

---

patrol: *guard and protect*
weaving: *stitching*

wrap up

Imagine you are a worker ant. Write a journal entry that describes all the different jobs you did on a 12-hour shift starting at 7:00 AM.

Worker and Larva
This weaver ant is using silk to glue the leaves together. The ant squeezes the larva, like a tube of glue, to produce the silk.

Amy's MEALWORM TACOS

By Amy Cousin

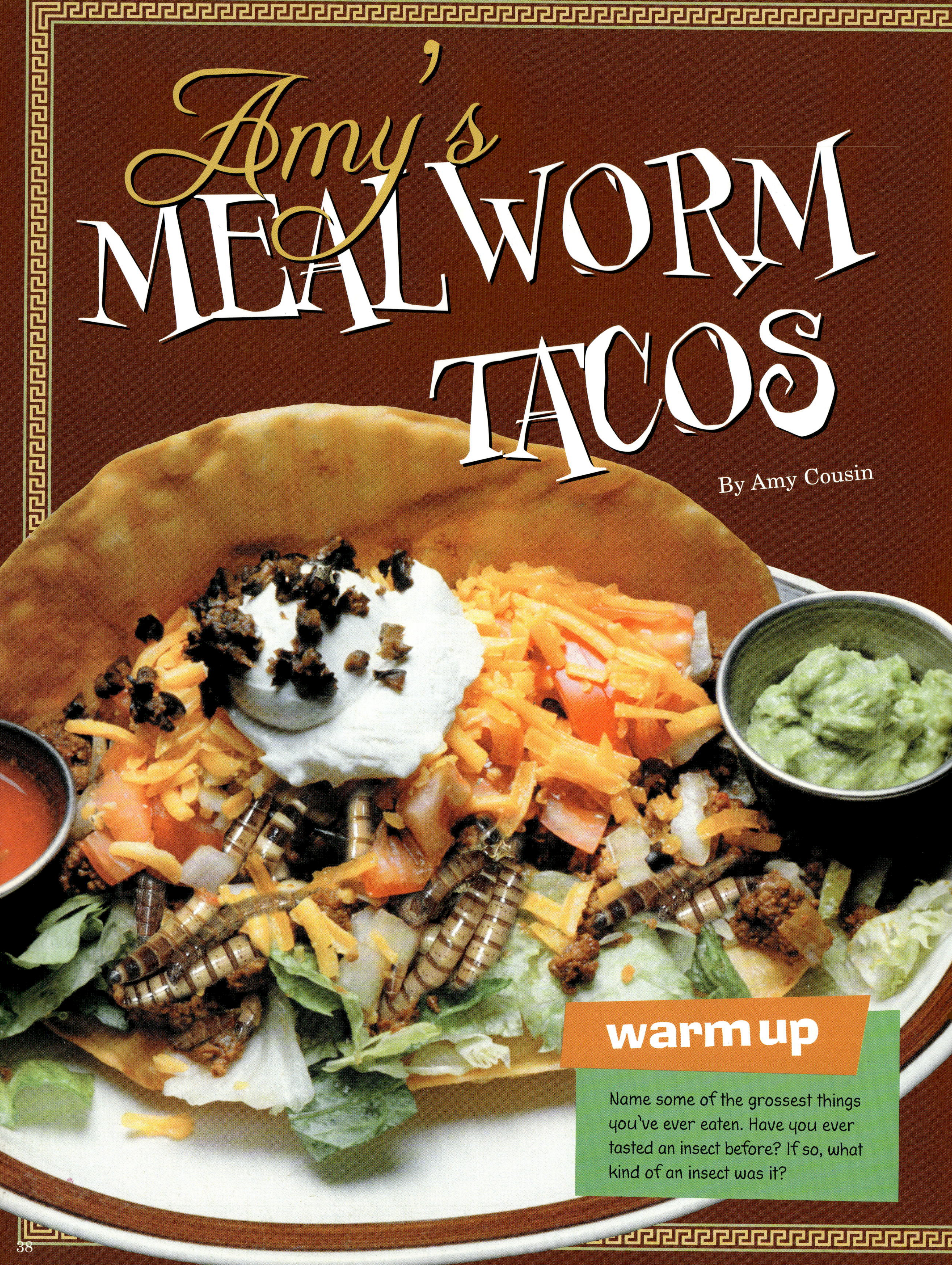

warm up

Name some of the grossest things you've ever eaten. Have you ever tasted an insect before? If so, what kind of an insect was it?

What You Need

* 2 tablespoons butter
* 1/2 pound cleaned mealworms
* 1 onion, finely chopped
* 3 serrano chilies, raw, finely chopped
* 1 tomato, finely chopped
* 1 packet of taco seasoning mix
* Taco shells, to serve

Steps

* Heat the butter in a frying pan and fry the mealworms
* Add the chopped onion, chilies, and tomato
* Sprinkle taco seasoning over mixture and gently stir to heat through
* Serve in taco shells

---

serrano chilies: *very hot chilies*

Taco–Getty Images/12282; Taco Toppings–Getty Images/48294

wrap up

Think of a dish you really like. Rewrite the recipe replacing food items with insects. You could pretend the "insects" represent real food — for example, raisins could represent ants or rice could represent maggots.

WEB CONNECTIONS

On the Internet find information about "**edible insects**" and the health benefits of eating these tiny creatures.

How Much Lunch Can a Caterpillar Munch?

By David Suzuki & Barbara Hehner

warm up

What food comes to mind when you are hungry? Think of three choices and compare your list with a friend's.

Just how much can a hungry caterpillar eat in one day? You can find out with some graph paper.

What You Need:

a caterpillar
a jar with a screen lid
a plant for the caterpillar to eat
2 pieces of graph paper

What To Do:

1. Find a caterpillar and put it in a jar. You need the right kind of food for your caterpillar. Many of them eat only one kind of plant. Very likely the plant on which you find the caterpillar is the food it likes. Bring home a branch of this plant.

2. Use a piece of graph paper with small squares. Lay the plant on the paper. Carefully, without hurting the plant, trace all its leaves onto the paper. Your graph paper should now look like the drawing.

Step 2

---

trace: *draw*

3. Put the plant in the jar with the caterpillar. Put the jar in a place out of direct sunlight. Leave the caterpillar alone for one day so that it can eat as much as it wants.

4. Count the squares on your graph paper that are covered by plant leaves. If a square is less than half covered, don't count it. If it is more than half covered, count it as a whole square.

5. After a day, take the plant out of the caterpillar jar. The leaves probably have lots of holes in them. Lay all the leaves on the second piece of graph paper. (Its squares have to be the same size as the ones on the first piece you used.) Trace around them. If there are holes in the middle of the leaves, trace around the holes too.

6. How many squares do the leaves cover now? Subtract the number of squares the munched leaves cover from the number that the fresh leaves cover. The difference is the amount the caterpillar ate. Let's work out the math with this example:

area of the fresh leaves	0.25 sq. in.
area of the chewed leaves	0.17 sq. in.

How many square inches of leaf did the caterpillar eat in one day?

0.25 sq. in. - 0.17 sq. in. = 0.08 sq. in
Try it with your caterpillar and see if it eats this much.

7. Think about how much salad you might eat for lunch.
Think about how big you are.
Think about how small the caterpillar is, and how much "salad" it ate. Are you impressed by its appetite?

8. Put the caterpillar back where you found it.

Step 6

wrap up

From your experiment, predict how many squares of leaf your caterpillar will eat in a week. Share your results with a friend.

Background Image–istockphoto

warm up

Have you seen bugs smashed on the windshield of a car? Are there more bugs in the country than in the city? Why?

Have you ever wondered how many bugs there are buzzing and screeching out there?

Is there a reason to count how many bugs there are in an area?

Scientists at the Royal Society for the Protection of Birds (RSPB) in England think so. Why? Well, birds feed on bugs. And if the bug population grows smaller, then there will be fewer dinners for hungry birds! Result? Fewer birds!

CHECKPOINT

Why are insects so important to birds?

How would we ever count those little critters? The clever RSPB scientists have created something called the "splatometer" to do the job.

The splatometer is made up of two pieces of clear sticky plastic. Before a trip, drivers stick one piece of the clear plastic to the front license plate or bumper of a car. As they drive along, insects splat and are stuck on the plastic sheet. At the end of the trip, drivers cover the splatometer with the other piece of sticky plastic.

Then, the drivers count and record the number and type of "splats" (splattered and smooshed insects) stuck on the splatometer. Easy!

In 2004, RSPB asked drivers from all over England to test the splatometer. Over 40,000 people took part in the survey and collected "splat information."

Scientists used computers to study the data. They counted a total of 324,814 splattered bugs. There was one "splat" taking place every 5 miles!

This information showed which areas had fewer insects than others. What do you think scientists will do next?

wrap up

1. Explain to a friend how the splatometer works.
2. In a small group, think of three other reasons for collecting splat information. Compare your reasons with those from another group.

All Images–istockphoto

Tuna Bugwiches

By Donna Bartolini

warm up

Have you ever helped an adult cook a meal? What did you do? What did you have to be careful about?

EQUIPMENT LIST

* Can opener
* Sieve
* Medium bowl
* Fork
* Cutting board
* Sharp knife
* Bread knife
* Cheese grater
* Dry measuring cups
* Spoon
* Rubber spatula
* Lemon juicer
* Measuring spoons
* Bread knife
* Vegetable peeler

CHECKPOINT

Do you know what all these kitchen tools are used for? If not, check with your teacher.

MAIN INGREDIENTS

8 dinner rolls
1/4 English cucumber thinly sliced
2 carrots
16 small lettuce leaves
Vegetable pieces

TUNA SALAD FILLING

3 cans (each 6.5 oz) water packed tuna
6 radishes
3/4 cup bread-and-butter pickles, chopped
1/2 cup light mayonnaise
1 tbsp lemon juice
1/2 tsp salt

Note: Ask an adult to help you make these delicious bugwiches.

Cutting Board–Getty Images OS48069; All other images–istockphoto

CHECKPOINT

Notice how the different ingredients help shape the insect.

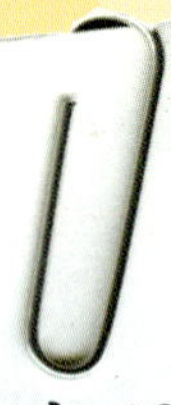

1. TUNA SALAD FILLING: Open cans of tuna. Place sieve over bowl; dump tuna into sieve to drain. Discard liquid; dump tuna into bowl. Using fork, break apart into small pieces.

2. Lay radishes on cutting board. With a sharp knife, trim off tops and roots neatly. Grate on medium holes of grater. Add to tuna along with pickles, mayonnaise, lemon juice, and salt. Mix well with fork: set aside.

3. Place rolls on cutting board. With bread knife, slice 1/2 inch from bottom. With fingers, pull out crumbs from top half, leaving 1/2 inch thick walls.

4. Place cucumber slices over bottom pieces of rolls; spoon on filling to make mounds. Cover with tops.

5. Peel carrots; cut into thick sticks about 3 inches long. You will need 48 sticks. Both the filled buns and carrots can be made to this point. Wrap buns separately and enclose carrot sticks in clean, damp towel in plastic bag. Refrigerate for up to 4 hours.

6. Insert carrot sticks into filling for legs. Make two slits, one on each side of the top of the roll; insert lettuce leaves for wings. Decorate with vegetable pieces for eyes, antennae, and other body parts. Use mayonnaise to attach.

* Makes 8 sandwiches.

Discard: *throw away*

Note Pad and Measuring Cups–istockphoto; Bugwiches–Photographed by Vincent Noguchi

wrap up

1. With help from an adult, follow the instructions and make a bugwich. Report on how it looked and tasted.

2. Create your own "bugwich" using ingredients of your choice. Write a recipe for your creation. Share it with your friends.

WEB CONNECTIONS

In some parts of the world, people eat real insects. For a taste of insect recipes from around the world, visit **http://www.frogsonice.com/froggy/recipes.shtml.**

ACKNOWLEDGMENTS

The publisher gratefully acknowledges the following for permission to reprint copyrighted material in this book.

Every reasonable effort has been made to trace the owners of copyrighted material and to make due acknowledgment. Any errors or omissions drawn to our attention will be gladly rectified in future editions.

Donna Bartolini: "Tuna Bugwiches" from *Canadian Living's Best Kids In the Kitchen*, published by Madison Press Inc. in association with Transcontinental Publications Inc. © 1998. Reprinted with permission from Donna Bartolini.

Amy Cousin: "Amy's Mealworm Tacos" from Sirius Mind and Body © 1999-2003. Permission courtesy of Amy Cousin.

Kij Johnson: "Why I Don't Brush My Teeth Anymore." Permission courtesy of Kij Johnson.

Tracy Trimpe: "Bug Jokes" from http://sciencespot.net. Permission courtesy of Tracy Trimpe.

"Investigate Ants" from INVESTIGATES: ANTS Published in 2000. Reprinted by permission of Random House Australia.

"Spot the Bugs in this Pond," reproduced from *Great Wildlife Search* by permission of Usborne Publishing, 83-85 Saffron Hill, London EC1N 8RT, UK. Copyright © 1998, 1996, 1995, 1994 Usborne Publishing Ltd.